KINGFISHER
READERS

level
1

Jobs
People Do

Thea Feldman

D0543958

KINGFISHER

J 331.7

🦅 KINGFISHER

First published 2012 by Kingfisher
an imprint of Macmillan Children's Books
a division of Macmillan Publishers Limited
20 New Wharf Road, London N1 9RR
Basingstoke and Oxford
Associated companies throughout the world
www.panmacmillan.com

Series editor: Heather Morris
Literacy consultant: Hilary Horton

ISBN: 978-0-7534-3318-8
Copyright © Macmillan Publishers Ltd 2012

9 8 7 6 5 4 3 2 1

1TR/1011/WKT/UNTD/105MA

A CIP catalogue record for this book is available from the British Library.

Printed in China

Picture credits
The Publisher would like to thank the following for permission to reproduce their material. Every care has
been taken to trace copyright holders. However, if there have been unintentional omissions or failure to trace
copyright holders, we apologize and will, if informed, endeavour to make corrections in any future edition.
Top = t; Bottom = b; Centre = c; Left = l; Right = r
Cover Photolibrary/ Index Stock Imagery; Pages 3cl Corbis/Edward Bock; 3cr Shutterstock (SS)/Monkey
Business Images; 3bl Corbis/Angel Wynn/Nativestock; 3br Corbis/Kelly-Mooney Photography; 4 SS/iofoto;
5 Corbis/LWA-Dann Tardif; 6 SS/Stephen Coburn; 7 Photolibrary/White; 8 Photolibrary/White; 9 Corbis/Richard
T. Nowitz; 10 SS/CandyBoxPhoto; 11 Photolibrary/White; 12 Corbis/Patrick Lane/Somos Images; 13 Corbis/Ariel
Skelley/Blend Images; 14 SS/OtnaYdur; 15 Corbis/Anderson Ross/Blend Images; 16 Alamy/Blend Images;
17 Alamy/fStop; 18 Alamy/Steve Skjold; 19 Photolibrary/Cuboimages; 20 SS/Lars Christiansen; 20b Corbis/Marc
Mueller/dpa; 21 Photolibrary/Bios; 22–23 Getty/NASA; 24 Photolibrary/ Index Stock Imagery; 25 Photolibrary/
Index Stock Imagery; 26 Getty/Michael Steele; 27 Photolibrary/Imagebroker; 28 SS/Lurii Osadchi; 29 SS/Igor
Bulgarin; 30tr Corbis/Paul Burns; 30cl Alamy/Blend Images; 30b SS/Kurhan; 31c SS/pistolseven;
31b SS/Denis Sabo.

It is a busy day.

People are working.

They are doing their jobs.

What are some jobs people do?

There are many jobs
in your town.

A **teacher** does one job
you know.

A teacher helps
children learn
many things.

You know the job a **postman** does too.

A postman brings letters to your home.

This person helps build
new homes.

These people help
other people move house.

Police officers work
to keep your town safe.

Firefighters put out fires.

They keep the town safe too.

A **doctor** in your town helps
sick people feel better.

This doctor helps
sick animals
feel better.

She is called a **vet**.

There are many jobs in the shops in town too.

A **grocer** sells food for your family to eat at home.

Someone adds up the prices
so your family can pay.

Do you like to eat
in a restaurant?

The cook
is called
a **chef**.

What is this
chef making?

Someone brings
your food.

Yum!

Why would you go to this shop?

To get a haircut, of course!

At the flower
shop, someone
sells flowers
and plants.

A bus driver drives the school bus.

A taxi driver takes
people where they
need to go.

A **pilot** flies an aeroplane.

A pilot's job takes him
far from home.

There are more jobs
that happen far from home.

This person studies animals
where the animals live.

An **astronaut** works
in space to help us
learn about it.

An astronaut's job is
really far from home!

A farmer's job is where he lives.

He lives in a house on a farm.

A farmer may plant food,
such as corn.

He may have cows
and chickens.

Some jobs may not look
like work.

But they are!

Football players work
hard to win a game.

Goal!

A zookeeper feeds the animals at the zoo.

People in a band play music.

They work hard to sound good!

A dancer does her job
on a stage.

There are so many jobs
people do.

What do you want to do
when you grow up?

Is it in this book?

Glossary

astronaut someone who works in space

chef someone who cooks in a restaurant

doctor someone who helps sick people get well

firefighter someone who puts out fires

grocer someone who works in a grocery store

pilot someone who flies an aeroplane

police officer someone who keeps your town or neighbourhood safe

postman someone who delivers the post

teacher someone who helps you learn many things

vet a doctor who helps sick animals get well